Ewan's Tale
A Valley Song

By

John Evans

I Erin, Gwyn ac Osian a phawb sy'n meiddio hedfan.

Table of Contents

Chapter 1

The Chicken and The Road

They were hard times, they were good times, they were no times at all, nobody went short, so you'll probably not want to listen to my joyful tale. No Angela's misery this, no gut wrenching story of sorrow and pain - at least not the dripping sort that those other sorry Celts tell - of cripples and dying dogs, orphans and starving mothers, bad sad fathers with no real passion in their bones. The gall of it, the credentials of those people to tell a melancholy tale. No, I've no sad tale to tell.

No choirs or collieries, no rugby how's your father, or *How Green Was My Valley* political hwyl; just lives, ordinary lives, ordinary people, not posh, but good, kind, house tidy, three times a day chapel people, some lapsed, living their lives as best they can, through the end of an era, with dreams, such dreams, and no shortage of bitter memories, and disappointments too.

But I've no sad tale to tell, even when the shadows fall and we talk of daft, mad, flew off the roof with a bucket on his head, Dafydd Ewan, and of loved ones lost. Mam, doll tiny, tough as a diamond, soft as an angel, ground from the country to work till she died with tireless, unerring devotion to her children and everyone else except her own lonely soul. And Dad, massive, rock like, mind and wisdom to match, Welsh to the marrow, mined from the valleys for the valleys, front of house grocer, miner in his day; driven, never single minded, by dreams of how much better his neighbours', his people's, his country's lot, ought to be; and by love, for family, friends, and community, loyally served, to a tragic, sad, but never bitter end. His life and the valleys, inextricably intertwined. We'll not weep. That wasn't his way. I've no sad tale to tell, but a fine, glad, happy story, first, of the beginning of the day.

....

I was there when the chickens died. Well, not quite. The fox was there when the chickens died. I just helped clear up the mess. At least I helpfully held back the flowers for my brother to dig the grave. August 15th, 1958. I was six, my brown eyed, look alike bossy from birth sister Sian, seven, and brainy brother Ieuan, a miles away eight, our minds never to meet till we were at least twenty two and too old to care. We was there. So was Dafydd Ewan, six and half, twp as a doormat and my best friend, HE was everywhere.

"You did shut the gate last night then Dafydd when you collected the eggs?" whispered Mam gently.

"Yes Mrs Davies, they were snug Mrs Davies, I wouldn av left the gate open Mrs Davies, the fox might ave um Mrs Davies."

"OK Dafydd, I'm sure you did mean to …" sighed Mam despairingly as we shut our eyes and pretended to pray. And then we sang, the only hymn that we all three knew, 'Onward Christian Soldiers...'

We were gutted, we were stricken, they were our friends, our family, our Christmas day dinner, our egg collecting task for the day; but we knew, three times a day chapel certain we knew, that we'd see them again, in eaven, though never sure how old they'd be, if they'd still be laying eggs, or which bit of paradise their coop would be in.

"Do yew think theyll get eaten in eaven Mrs Davies?" chirped Dafydd inquisitively. "Does God eat chickins …?"

"I don't think so Dafydd, I don't think God, or Jesus, eats chickens."

"What about John Baptist Mrs Davies? He'd eat anythin, Mrs Davies ..."

"Dafydd! The chickens are in safe hands, go and play."

We ran, to the security of our bottom of the garden den, the chickens gone, and forgotten for at least forty years.

We had moved, you see, radically up market, from the tiny, hill clinging, one bedroomed stone cottage, to the top of the hill concrete and stone, main road bungalow, its name, 'Heddfan', 'Peace', where none ever was to be found; two separate bedrooms, stamp size kitchen, a sitting room nobody was ever allowed to sit in and a toilet INDOORS … with pull and flush chain, and garden too … all set in soon to disappear cow fields licking the terraces where

Dafydd and all our other friends played. Two thousand pounds worth of paradise courtesy of Tadcu, Dad's dad, on a loan interest free. We were kings, we had arrived. With a garden the size of Ponty everyone would be our friends. And there was a van: tank grey, money box square, speed of a tortoise, noise of a growling bulldog, the biggest that Pendre had ever before seen … at least in our tiny eyes.

It was Bopa's doing, bless her. She had died, 'suddenly', Dad said, 'in the middle of the night when she was asleep', which I always thought a pity, been as I bet she'd have wanted to know, leaving the milk round and tiny, stock everything, front room grocer's shop, for Dad to run. His pit days over, we could relish the prospect of seeing him white. No more counting his steps up the pavement to the safety of him home, no more Mam scraping coal of his back scarred black, and best of all, 'No more paying for sweets,' said Ewan, now that we had a shop, or 'Using our legs now that we could travel in a van.'

"We'll ide in the back," said Ewan one fine Saturday morning, "yer … under the potato sacks, ee wun mind, ee wun know till we get to Pendre Fach then it'll be too late to turn back an eell have to take us to the shop and give us a Milky Way to go ome … Come on Rhys, eell be out in a minit."

The two miles to Dad's new shop edged wearily down a narrow, winding road and Dad, always home on Saturdays in those days to kiss Mam and have dinner, was ready to leave. And on Saturdays, Ewan was always dangerously bored. "Less ide in the van Rhys … get a ride … it'll be good … ee won know … ees a bit def … get in … come on … eisht … Lie down still or eell see you … you cretin, ees comin."

Lying flat on the cold dirt covered floor of Dad's precious van we pulled the sacks over our heads and playing dead we waited … until the door slammed and with a shuddering jerk and one of Dad's crackling woodbine coughs we were off, heading with certainty for Pendre and the mouth-watering possibility of a penny Milky Way. But as we rattled downwards and nearing Pont bend, the sack dust rose and flew its sun drenched flecks up Ewan's drizzling nose. He sneezed, farting simultaneously, the devil's trumpet, the snot and dust hitting Dad's dashboard like shite from Tonto's horse. "Mercy Mawr bachgen!!! Wos going on!!!" swore Dad as he swerved, lost control, veered off the road and into the roadside hedgerow like a mole down a hole. And as the van lurched to a shuddering halt the van back doors flew open and Ewan leapt out, into the nettled hedgerow and off back up Pendre hill.

"Sorry Dad," I whimpered, running my hand over the bonnet of his badly bruised van. "We ony thought we'd hitch a ride with yew to work see ... for a

Milky Way. Didn' mean to frightn yew. Will the van work again Dad? Yew can't see the dent much Dad."

As he pulled the branches and heather from the bonnet of his badly bruised van, Dad's silence scraped the skin of my bum. "That boy Rhys ... Duw, he could be bad for Wales that un. God help im I say, and yew, when I get you home. Give us a push bach, what's done's done now, the shop's waiting ... I suppose yew meant no harm. Push, push ... but yew can forget your trip to the bloomin Miky Way."

We didn't talk much of the van after that. Ewan said we were lucky to be alive and that my Dad could ave killed us with iss wild drivin, and it was good anyway seeing we wouldn't lose the use of our legs now that we couldn't go near the van and had to walk everywhere. Ewan was banned, I was grounded, for as long as it took to repair the van, a fortnight, a lifetime in our time.

It was then, I think, that Ewan decided that it would be better if we could fly.

Chapter 2

Matters of Flying

"I saw it on the telly in Rediffusion Rhys," said Ewan, the first Saturday back from solitary. "No kiddin, they ad wings strapped to their arms, jumped off a bridge they did, silly buggers. They was useless. Too evy the lot of them, should ave used babies, they'd ave gone up, you know how them little tots flap their arms. We could do it, specially fore dinner, we'd be light then, bound to go up ... an we'll win sum money." Ewan was confident, I was certain, it was all a matter of weight, planning and finding the right bits to make the wings work. "Thosll do," said Ewan, pointing to the side panels of the old Welsh dresser that Dad had brought from the cottage and stored in the garage before moving it inside. "We cun put it back together after, yewr not going to use it, an anyrate iss old and got woodworm. If we fly we'll be on the tele an get loads of money an yewr Dadll be able to buy a new wun, so yewr Mamll be happy. Anyway theyre already loose, this wuns nearly off."

With a crunching wrench Ewan tore the first of the panels from the dresser's side, the other followed with a similar sickening groan. "Find some string Ewan ... we'll need some string to tie um to yewr arms, an some plasters just in case it goes wrong." Undaunted by this nagging doubt Ewan searched the garage for string. "This'll do," he said, dragging free the yellow brittle rope holding shut the coal shed door. "Tie this on me tight Rhys. I dun wan my wings movin about wen I'm up there. This is a good idea Rhys ..."

With wings like windmills strapped tightly to his drooping arms, Ewan edged slowly, unsteadily, upwards, towards the garage roof. "We should ave tied um on when we was up there Rhys … iss ard on this ladder … balancing no arms."

"No, iss better this way, too much trouble when yewr up there … an keep goin … yewr bums on my ed … Dew look at that Ewan … is not very long … not much of a runway," I said, scanning the short stretch of corrugated roof now shaking perilously beneath our weight. "Ewan, yewve got t sprint … fast as a spitfire … or yew'll never get nough speed up to take off, an don forget to jump up at the end. Yew wanna go up not down. Don go yet though, I'll get a bucket. Yewll need a bucket. If yew hit a pylon when yewr up there yewll need someut on yer ed, and don't stay up too long, I wana av a go after you, Mamll be back soon, I've got to go in for dinnu at twelve."

Blinded by the bucket and slowed by his drooping, leaden, outstretched arms, Ewan lurched forward like a giant locust stumbling blind and battered from recently sprayed corn … gradually building to an unsteady drunken trot … until … with bucket rattling … Ewan leapt … He was launched.

Mam said the trees shook all over Pendre when Ewan hit the ground. I said he should have jumped better and not been greedy and eaten Welsh cakes minutes before the launch. Ewan said the bucket adn elped im an anyway we should ave ad longer grass to cushin his fall. The hospital said he was lucky, the damage to his legs wasn permanent and nobody would notice the bruises to his brain. Dad said if he couldn't put the dresser back together Ewan wouldn't live to see a day over ten.

"Not what yewd expect," said Ewan dejectedly, "from a deesunt chapel going man."

Chapter 3

The Horse

"I'm bored," said Ewan the following Saturday as we sat on the wood piles that passed for a boundary between our house and Pritchard Jenkins coal. "Bloodee bored," he repeated, practising the language that he said he got from his ugly sister Joan. "There's nothing to do round yer and my legs are gettin short. Iss yer Dad's fault we're not tall, if eed let us in the van we wouldn ave to walk. We need an orse, we could do things with a orse."

Never less than specific about the nature of our needs Ewan continued, "Ask yewr Mam, Rhys, tell er we need a orse to make us grow … yewr Dad wun mind, tell im it'll be good for iss cabbages, an e can sell the van. Tell im we could do things wi a orse."

"Where we gonna get a orse from Ewan?" I said seriously, "an a saddle," further weighing up the merits of his latest greatest plan. "They cost a bomb, an we've ony dun the donkees at Aber, we don know ow to ride wun."

"Bare back," said Ewan, undeterred, "like Tonto on the tele … seasy, just ang on to is air and yu bounce, and Uncle Jack'll get us a good un down the knackers yard, a tenner, he told me, for a racer like Silver, though might not be that same colour. We could be the Lone Ranger and Zorro ..."

"Tonto, Ewan," I interrupted.

"Ony difference," he went on, "we'd have to take turns ridin im, or sit on im in a row."

I needed no more convincing. This was Ewan's finest plan.

We could do things with a orse.

That night, with Dad front of fire puffing woodbines like Popeye, Sian and Ieuan fighting like ferrets over marmite and burnt toast and Mam busy making Welsh cakes tellin tales of Gran's troubles with Cariad the rat catching farm cat - "wouldn't burn, even when she stoked it with a shovel she said it wouldn't burn, must ave been out in the rain. Lord above, I hope it was dead when she put it on, God rest its soul, she shouldn't be liftin cats her age anyway" - I delicately broached the matter of me an Ewan's urgent need for a orse.

"We need a orse Mam," I blurted in my most polished grown up voice. "Ewan said it'll be good for our elth and the cabbagis, an it'll keep the grass down, we'll keep it down Cwm … Gransha said, s'long as we feed it once a day we could av one, it'd keep us out of trouble, we need a orse."

The speech, though long, had clearly struck home. Dad's woodbine drooped dangerously from the side of his mouth and Ieuan and Sian ceased fighting mid flow.

"Yeah Dad," chirped Ieuan and Sian in harmony getting into the flow and spotting another of Ewan's daft dreams. "Ee needs a orse, it'll keep Tiddles warm, the cat needs a friend, we can keep im in er basket."

Dad laid back on his chair and took a long draw.

"Mercy mawr bach, a horse, what d'y need a horse for, what will he think of next eh? Dafydd Ewan said, did e? And where does Dafydd think we're going to get a horse from or the money to pay for im, it don grow on trees."

"Ewan's brains does," interrupted Ieuan unhelpfully.

"We're not havin a horse goin all over the lawn," continued Dad.

"I'll use my milk-round money Dad," I pleaded. "I'll pay a fiver and I'll pay yew back the rest, Ewan's Uncle Jack knows were to get one cheap, says they ony cost a tennu from the knackers, thas reely good Dad."

"The knackers eh," chuckled Dad beaming, his half finished woodbine glowing red as he took another draw. "Yeah Ewan's Uncle Jack saves um from having their knackers off, Ewan said it would be a blessin for the orse if we ad one Dad, a real good deed."

Dad laughed, "They wont need their knackers bach if they're at the knackers yard, and never yew mind what Ewan says, we're not having a horse to save his or Ewan's balls."

"That's enough Glyn," chirped Mam. "I don't know where he learns to speak like that. The boy's serious, you know they're daft as brushes once they've got an idea in their heads, so don't encourage them, tell them No, we can't be having horses on the lawn."

"Orse Mam," I corrected, hopelessly, spotting a lost cause.

"I don't know what Gransh was thinking. I'll put im right tomorrow," murmured Mam.

"Nice idea bach, but they're a lot of trouble and we can't afford one," said Dad kindly, "and you heard what your mother said, so don't give it a second thought, and don't listen to Ewan, ees as daft as a donkey himself."

Half past ten the following Saturday, Dafydd Ewan unusually absent from our back yard, the horse arrived. Thirteen hands of dog meat with madness in its eyes. Mam screamed, "Diawlch Rhys, get out yer at once there's a orse on the lawn, get it off right now or you're straight to bed. Is this yewr doing, or Ewan's, need I ask?"

I ran to the window and wiped my eyes - a stallion, 'Silver' we'd call him, by magic, had arrived.

"Yers yer orse missus," said Ewan's Uncle Jack, matter of fact, "as ordered. Lucky to get this un, Missus, nice beast, good runner, mannurs too, eats what e shits, a stunner, last for years, yewll love im, be a tenner for you and yew can av the reins chucked in, don pull um too ard, theys fragile. Just say woo an eell stop, when e wants, and don feed im carrots, makes im grumpy." And with that Jack tied the reins around Mam's outstretched fist-clenched hands and I shoved the fiver into Jack's well worn, mangy, horse chewed coat.

"That'll do nice for now Missus, I can cum back for the rest wen yur fixed, just leave Ewan a note and I'll be round."

With that, he was gone, leaving Mam, me, and Silver eating daisies, silent, on the lawn .... and Ewan, grinning, striding from the side of the coal shed doorway like Tonto off the plain. "Dew, iss a beaut Mrs Davies, a racer, looks like a lamb, yewll be pleased with that one then Mrs Davies, last yew years, yew can get the bread on im, gallup up the shops ... I spect yewll be keepin im in the chickins cot Mrs Davies."

With that, Mam groaned, from the bottom of her soul, and cried, obviously overjoyed. Grasping the moment, Ewan tugged the rope from Mam's hands, whacked the orse's backside, and beaming, led me and Silver away in the direction of Gransha's farm.

Later that sunny evening in the green fields of Cwm, Dad, from behind the safety of the old wooden gate nervously smoothed Silver's flea-bitten nose and laughed. "Duw it's Ewan's mongrel brother ... they must ave crossed im with the devil and a sheep or a ferret or was it a Caerphilly mountain goat to get this one. Yew hang on to im wen yewr on im mind ... doubt if ees been ridden for yers. Still, yew havn got far to fall ees no bigger than a mole." And from beneath his woollen brown green balaclava, Ewan heaved a deep sigh of relief and whispered seriously, "Rhys, yewr Dad reely luvs im. You think eell wanna swop im for the van?"

Chapter 4

Shitin in the Bucket

"We'll show im," said Ewan suddenly, and emphatically, the following day, as he pulled his sister's pink hairbrush roughly and repeatedly through Silver's mud matted tail, "next Saturday, Maerdy fair, orse show, bound to win, we'll show im in the best orse bit o the show. Look at the air on im … av yew ever seen an airier orse? Iss air an the colour o the eyes that counts. We'll hose im down and cut iss tale to make im look posh and well show im … bound to win. We'll split the winins for chips and the flix, Dracla's sister's on."

Fired with the certainty of money in our pockets and seeing Dracla at the flix, we pulled vigorously and recklessly at Silver's tangled mane, leaving clumps of grey black bristles from Ewan's sister's hairbrush and Silver's thinning hair, mingling with the chickens' mornings droppings carpeting Gransha's grey, cold, cow-shed floor.

It was three miles from Pendre to Maerdy top through the terraced streets of Pont Fach and Pentregoch, the quickest route, according to Dafydd Ewan, along the narrow main road. "I'll lead" he said, "eell be oright if we old im tight … I can owld im better than yew, I know orses … yew can ould the buckit."

"Buckit … What buckit!?" I replied in tortured surprise, "whadawe need a buckit for … ?!"

"To clean up the shite," retorted Ewan. "Jack says yew've got to clean up behind the orse or the coppers av ew, an eel give us thruppence a load for his roses if iss good solid stuff."

"We'll take it in turns then," I snapped defiantly, deep down knowing that I would be following Silver and watching his oversized backside.

"Need to be there by leven," said Ewan, "if we're gona get im in a good position. We'll av to leave by nine. Won take long though, I spect eell want t gallup most of the way."

Half past eight the following Saturday, with Silver hosed and tail cut short - "thas wot they do Rhys when you show um" - we set off from Pendre farm on the road to Pont Fach. Ewan confidently led the way, me following nervously with bucket at ready a few steps behind. As we made our way out of Pendre, up the old school road towards Pont Fach Ewan tugged impatiently on the wafer thin string reins as Silver, two hooves shoeless, limped and laboured slowly behind him like a broken rocking horse, all the while hugging the hedgerow along the narrow winding road. "Don seem to wanu go very fast today," said Ewan tugging on the reins impatiently. "Praps ees jus warming up."

"Make him go faster then," I pleaded desperately, praying inwardly that none of our friends would see me and bucket catching droppings cascading from Silver's bum. "Get im to urry up Ewan, ees goin too slow an ees got dyarea … this stuffs no good for Jack's roses."

With tail tied high and plagued by his new inability to swot horseflies from his badly bitten bum Silver was in no mood for either speed or fun. "Seems as grumpy as yew are today," said Ewan. "Yewd think eed be yewsd to flies by now wouldn ew, ees been round long unuf, an I hope yewr daft Gransha didn give im carrots in iss orses special puddin this mornin, ees lively enuf as it is and we don wan im fartin and shitin any more at the show wen were showin im do we."

As we walked past the terraced streets of Pendre Fach, Silver's frustration at having no tail and a growing distaste for the morning's stroll was becoming increasingly intense. "Wo Silver, wo o boy," said Ewan soothingly, confident that he still had control, "save it for the show boy, wo oo."

The coal board lorry that singed past Slver's ears was, for Silver, the last brittle straw. As it spewed noise and dust into his and our eyes, Silver's body shuddered, majestically, like one of Ewan's practised classroom fits. Eyes blazing, he threw his head back, snorted like a wart hog, and bolted, the reins slipping Ewan's hands like water off a pole. "Dew, look at the bugger go," spluttered Ewan as we chased after him, hopelessly, up Pont Street. "Ees better thun a greyhound … bound to win … ees like a pig out of ell."

"Ya twp bugger Dafydd," I shouted back, less enamoured by Silver's turn of speed than the sight of his bum fast disappearing around Pont bend. "Whyd yew let im go you cretin, I knew yew should av been oldin the buckit, how we gonna catch im now?"

"Don panic, ees got to stop," panted Ewan, "wen e gets to Top street, carn go no further, mountains in the way … we'll get im there, as long as e don go in ole Joe's allotment we'll be alright, we'll soon ave im back on the road. I hopes ees not got dirty, mind, else we'll never win im in the show."

Although old Joe had been retired from the colliery for over two years, his dedication to his prized allotment had done very little to mellow his sad and angry soul. "Iss the dust that got im retired and puts im in a bad mood," said Dad kindly one Sunday tea time as he tried to explain old Joe's distinctly un-Christian attitude towards people, all creatures small and Preece Pritchard's lame dog Cassidy in particular. "Fired more likely he was," interrupted Mam, less charitably. "Nobody would work with the awful man, ees God gifted cussed and naturally mean, and old Cass carn help going on his plot - he carn walk far. Anyway, iss droppings is good for Joes beans."

"An e strangls cats ans cruel to kids," chipped in Sian, helpfully,

"Too right Mrs Davies," said Ewan authoritatively, mouth full of cake and sandwich, "good as dead if yew as much look at iss radishes or touch iss broad beans. Jack says is iss piles that makes Joe nasty."

It was clear, if Silver landed in Joe's allotment plot, one of us was dead. I felt convinced it should be Ewan.

We were dead.

Silver had stopped and had settled to graze, languidly, against old Joe's allotment shed. "Jesus elp us Dafydd," I gasped, "how we gonna get im out o there and live?"

"No worries," said Ewan, "Joes probly sleepin, ee ony cums out at night … wait yer, but if yew see me do this," Ewan pulled vigorously at the front of his balaclava, "come out coffin with a limp." With that and the look of the Lone Ranger striding down the high road to settle an old score, Ewan made his way towards old Joe's allotment plot.

"Jeessus don let im be there," I prayed as Ewan sidled past the allotment shed to where Silver now grazed, oblivious to the gathering storm clouds that were just about to break…

"Is that yewr orse boy?' thundered Joe, evidently NOT sleeping, "yew and ees for the knackers if ees as much as touched my radishes, you little runt … Wos that lump of dog shite doin on my ground?"

"Ullo Mr Lewis" said Ewan politely in his best, once a month chapel voice, "didn see you there. Ows yewr coffin these days Mr Lewis? Jack says you should try smokin Mr Lewis, says it'll take yer mind of yewr piles."

"Ill take yer mind of it and yer ed if I get old of you … you little runt," he growled again. "Wos that ruddy lump of dog meat doing on my plot?"

"Ees not mine Mr Lewis, iss is over there," said Ewan pointing unnaturally to the side of his head and then to me limping and coughing from behind the garage wall. "Ees ad a nasty turn Mr Lewis, fell off is orse, said I'd catch it for im … ees invalidid Mr Lewis, if I dont get im back on the orse an ome for is tablets eel probly die, look there ee is now Mr Lewis," pointing to me again as I tripped over the strings connecting sticks to broad beans. "See, ees gona die on your leeks if we don urry." And with that, Ewan grabbed at what remained of Silver's dangling reins and yanked him away, leaving Joe, eyes ablaze, blood pressure rising dangerously, mouth agape, pondering whether to waste further obscenities on Silver's sick friends, or save what was left of his broken, horse trodden, broad beans.

With echoes of Joe's venom ringing in our ears, we ran, laughing, praying simultaneously. We were alive, Silver ambling, me leading, Ewan following with the bucket, on the road to Maerdy show.

"Iss yewr fault," said Ewan dejectedly as we reached Maerdy just in time to see the parade of horses leaving the center of the field. "The 'best orse' bit of the show's over."

"My fault! Yew should ave pulled im arder … howd yew expect me to make im go quicker if I'm shuvlin shite behind … an how we gonna see Dracla now?"

Ewan strode off towards the central office tent to assess the possibilities that remained for us to make money and Silver achieve fame, leaving me standing sheepishly in the midst of a slowly gathering crowd curious to see the contents of the bucket dangling from my hand.

"Is that a orse yew've got there then bach?" asked Gwilym Hughes, local farmer and expert on all matters meat, "or a caterpillar with legs? Pity yew missed the best orse bit of the show, wouldn ave been another like im in the ring."

"Wher've yew been Ewan?" I snapped angrily when he finally returned, with cucumber smile etched on his face. "I've been surrounded yer by bloomin ideuts wanin t know wot make of orse this is an why we're savin shite in a buckit."

"Iss orright," spat Ewan, ignoring my angry remonstration, "I've fixed it, ees in the 'point to point', bound to win."

"Jeessus wept, Ewan," I spluttered in disbelief, "you can't put im in the point to point, eel be slaughtered, eel be running against Walesis best, even Williams orse got his orse in the point to point."

"You saw im go up Pont Street," snarled Ewan unmoved by my shameful doubt. "Ees oviously got racers blood in im - once e gets going eel shift all em others out the way like a ferret down a rabbit ole. Ave yew seen um, those other orses … not a bit o meat or air on their arses, like Mrs Phillpot's rats."

"An whos gonna ride im then Ewan? An hows ee gonna stay on without a saddle eh, eel be killd!"

"I am," said Ewan emphatically, annoyed that the question should even have been asked. "Iss easy, all you do is get yer ed down and ang on to is air and he jus goes round, follows the other orses," forgetting the idea was to have Silver in front, "an iss ony twice round the field, eel wallop um."

The 'point to point' was the high point finale of Maerdy's annual horse fair and an important event in the racing calendar for the small-time horse owner farmers, plentiful in South Wales. To win was a major honour, not just for the horse but the farm, a mark of quality training, months of careful preparation and expert horse care.

With the sun shining satin on the saddled horses in the race, Ewan and Silver jostled for position, sandwiching themselves snugly between the thoroughbreds like a cockroach in caviar. Then, closing their eyes, Ewan waited, agonisingly, impatiently, straining beneath his balaclava, to hear the shouted ... 'GO'.

'Crack'... the gun fired, shaking crows from the track side oak trees like a whirlwind clearing leaves ... they were off!

Startled and with fear oozing every pore, Ewan and Silver, tail menacingly bent backwards in the direction of his ears, together leapt forward, incredibly, to the front of the raging queue, with a miraculous turn of speed.

"Dew," said Williams orse, "he must have the devil in im, or on im, ees a ruddy rockit wi hair."

With bum dancing dangerously, unnaturally mid air, heads blended, arms throttling and glued to Silver's streaky streaking hair, Ewan and horse, mad eyed and terrified by the pounding pack behind, hurtled forward, to the astonishment of the gasping crowd. He was leading... until the first bend.

"How was I to know ee couldn go round corners," said Ewan defiantly afterwards, "the daft bugger shoulduv known to turn left, ee ad is eyes open didn ee?"

While the galloping pack charged left to take the first bend of the course, Silver carried straight on, shot the steep banking and hurtled through the trees, down and out of the ringside field, the following applause wasted on Ewan's windswept backside and balaclavaed ears. "Ruddy fast," shouted Williams race orse, bent double with laughter, "but lacks direction. Jockey must be missing a screw or two if you ask me … an a saddle."

I found Ewan sitting dejectedly in a shallow ditch, precariously close to old Joe's allotment plot; bruised, battered but otherwise intact. "Yew did well Ewan, yew wer out in front for a bit … pity bout the bend though," I sighed encouragingly, trying to raise his dampened spirits. But Ewan neither wanted comfort, nor could be consoled. "Cheated, cheated we wos," he spluttered defiantly. "I was waitin for the daft man in the Dai cap to shout 'Go' not shoot a bloody gun. Wad he espect after eed frytnd the orse like that, twp bugger. It was a miracle nobody fell off an was ert, an anyway Silvers obviously a jumper, I spect he was looking for the jumps in the woods."

It was the end of Ewan's career as a jockey, and shortly after, of Silver's as a orse. Old, increasingly immobile, with the help of Ewan's Uncle, he made his last journey out of Pendre to join his tired butties at Morgan's knackers yard. "He was a good orse," said Ewan touchingly on the Sunday they took him away. "He wan no racer but ee could av been a jumpu, an in any case, ee got us into see Dracla's sister din ee, with the thrupence we got for the solid stuff he shite us from is arse."

Chapter 5

Prison Days

We hated school - nursery, primary, secondary - with the kind of passion born of terror of being thumped daily in our best interests by teachers - Wallace-mean, Lewis-nasty and worst of all the dreadful and dangerous 'my fingers are itchin' headmaster Mr Sade, none of whom in Dafydd Ewan's books, "Dracla would ave ad as friends." But our hatred of schools was matched equally by my and Ewan's soul saving, delirious, unremitting love for playtime, dinner and break times, moments to conjure fantasies of cowboys, knights in armour and endless football games, and play by a different, altogether nicer set of rules. "Whyd we aftu av lessons" snarled Ewan for the umpteenth time as we walked through the primary school gate, "we don need um, yew erd what Jack said, nevu did im enee good, all teachers are bloody yewslus n daft."

I couldn't help but agree.

My day began ritually at six thirty, to Mam's waking warning call, "Yew up Rhys? Eel be ere in half hour, get a move on." I hated the mornings, all mornings, but especially the crisp, cold, frost biting creeping sort that seeped through the crevices of my blankets, even when bound tightly around me like a mummy in a tomb, to gnaw relentlessly at my eyelids and the marrow of my bones. Oh how I hated them, just about as much as Mam loved them. And the earlier it was, the happier she was, and the happier she was the more miserable I became. "Do yew ave to be so appy Mam, don't yew like sleepin?" I would plead as she hummed 'Bright and Beautiful' for the umpteenth umpteenth time while raking embers from the hearth and carrying away the ashes from the fire she'd got blazing for us all. Dad, motionless as always at this time of day, saying nothing, his face, shaving soap white, glued to kitchen mirror, razor in hand ready to do mortal battle with the whiskers on his chin, knowing he wouldn't be leaving Heddfan without at least two pieces of blood-stained *South Wales Echo* dangling from gashes where once had been his skin. "Urry up Rhys," Mam would fuss as I wolfed down porridge, toast and butter and a cup of boiling tea. "He won wait for yew frever, you know wot ees like, an don't be late for school, don't go hangin about for that daft Ewan right, just go in."

Slinking slowly from the breakfast table, feet crunching brittle bits of toast an jam, I watched as Ieuan and Sian sank miserably into their chairs, each slumping, slowly, rubbing eyes, grunting, "mornin Mam" while ignoring my sullen parting, a mumbled hushed "good bye". With Dai cap covering eyelids and trench coat wrapped tightly around my coal fired warmed up bones, I pulled the door softly behind me and, head bowed, trudged slowly up Top Street to await on the frosty roadside, the jingle jangle milk crate arrival of Dai's rust red milk delivery van.

I had been given the job on Dai's milk round when twp two pints short of a puddin Geraint Morgan had moved to live with his Aunty Beryl and work on the donkeys at Porthmawr. Dad had said it would be good for me to do some proper work and Ieuan, that it was about time I did sumthin useful, been as ee'd been in the shop helpin Dad since before ee was born and it wasn as ard work as iss, since he ad to serve iss teacher Wallace-mean, an smile same time; while Sian kept quiet for fear of finding herself no longer unemployed. To be truthful, though I never let such honesty slip on Ieuan, I enjoyed the milk round as much as the money it provided to buy me and Ewan bangers for November 5th and sweets twice a day, especially once the frost had lifted from the bottle tops, the sun had kissed the ground good-bye and risen to breathe warmth to my fingertips and feeling to the ends of my toes.

"Oright Rhys?" mumbled Dai as my morning greeting, the only civil words I could expect except for 'two pints Mrs Lewis, dozen eggs', 'three pints Mrs Callow', when either I'd forgotten, or he thought I needed promptin to go quicker on my way.

"How comes I've always got to go up the steps and yew does the houses on the flat Dai?" I ventured one morning breaking the rule of silence, when, with the rain crashing down so heavily, I'd been released from my outside position of sitting parrot perched, legs dangling over the tail end of his van to join him, resting snug as a maggot warm and dry inside.

"Yewr fittu than me," snapped Dai sullenly, "and anyway it'll do yu legs good, when yewr my age you can do my calls if I'm retired appy."

There were exceptions.

Although Preece's greyhound had long lost the capacity to win races, he hadn't his desire for attacking anything that moved. "Ees a nice dog," Preece would say holding the dog's collar while Mince, froth seeping unpleasantly from his mouth like mouldy molten foam, strained to free himself from his owner's fragile hold, "just he confuses people for rabbits. Is iss eyes, not what they used to be, ee won urt yew if yewr nice t im."

It was the only house in Pendre, on the flat, to which Dai let me deliver milk. Yet despite the lack of gradient, it was the second longest and most hated delivery of the day.

"Mamll never forgiv yew Dai if she knew yew was makin me go in there, what if ee eats me, yewll av to go up the steps."

In fear of being mistaken for a rabbit and knowing that even if Mince did have bad eyes there was nothing at all the matter with his ears, teeth or sense of smell, I would quietly pray and advance tip toe, hugging my milk bottles like a miser caressing gold, convinced that even if Mince didn't hear the bottles rattle he'd feel the vibration of glass meeting concrete floor; or failing that catch a whiff of my musty morning smell, 'Fairy', mixed with fear … and aroused, he would be upon me, drooling, dripping blood, like a Werewolf in a bad Palace horror movie, to rip me limb from limb. On a good day Mince was caged; on a bad day, madly, rampaging out. This was a bad day.

With the look of a rabid werewolf with rabbits on his brain, Mince hurtled towards me with the speed of an out of control steam train. Dropping the bottles, I leapt, despairingly, downwards to the stone pathway below, to lie prone and helpless on the mud-covered cold stone floor. My strangled scream, "Dai ees got me," never reaching the safety of Dai seated comfortably in his nicely warmed up van. "Don worry luv … ees ony tryin to lick ew," soothed Mrs Preece as she darted out from the front door. "Best if yew don move though, an keep yewr ears coverd sos he don think yewr a rabbit ... There, there, lovely boy," she purred as she trailed the contents of her half finished box of *Black Magic* for Mince to eat instead of me. Mince weighed his options … sniffed, munched and moved languidly from my crumpled body back to the security of Preece's front door. "There yew are luv, eel be alright now. I don think yew've fritind im too much. Leave us two pints tomorrow will yew. I'm makin Preece a puddin," and with that she slammed the door.

"Urry up Rhys," Dai snapped when I got back to the van, dripping wet and white with fear. "What have yew been doing in there - playing pat u cake with the dog? I told yew not to bother im. Leave im alone next time."

Perched again on the back of van, we went quietly on our way.

Whether we arrived at Pendre junior the right side of the school day in time to meet Ewan and stroll together through the gates, heads bowed, or minutes after, leaving me alone to creep to assembly like a lamb to a dangerous lair, depended on the length of Dai's endless indoor chin-waggin chattin with Lloyd Preece's posh daughter Emily, who was never seen outside. It was always the last and longest call of the morning milk round, minute upon minute of brain numbing boredom while racked by cold and creeping fear of being dangerously late for Sade's assembly in front of all the school. "Needed someone to talk to," sighed Dai as he trudged cap in hand down the pathway quarter of an hour after having disappeared around the back with a pint. "Er mothers a bit fragile and Emily needs a friendly hand."

"Wot about my bloomin ands, I'm dyin out yer from the feet up," I grumbled, despairingly, fingers clasped, legs dancing to keep the morning cold from biting deeper into my re-frozen tingling bones.

With Dai comfortable inside the van we again headed to Pendre top, me balanced precariously on the tip end of the van, impatiently, ready to leap, the van slowing never stopping, as we passed the school gates.

With Ewan already in assembly, lost but for flagship brown balaclava pointing elf like upwards while smothering the majority of his head, I slithered between the subdued mass of swaying children sitting squashed, cross legged, on the yellow wooden parquet floor. Sidling quietly past the po faced sentry teachers leaning idly at each corner of the hall, I prayed despairingly that I'd escape Sade's fearful stare.

"Milkin cows again Rhys Davies, can't yew milk um a bit faster and get here quicker?!" snapped Mr Sade not breaking from his morning ministerial flow, and I slumped to huddle by Ewan, positioned yearningly close to the playground exit door,

"Ees reel grumpy today," whispered Ewan, "watch out ... Jack says iss Mams seriously ill and dyin, discovered ees her son an nuthin the doctu can do bout it."

"Something the matter with yew Davies?" stormed Mr Sade as I tried to stifle the chuckle rising in my throat. "STAND UP, and yew Ewan," he bawled, "if yew cant sit quiet you can't sit down, stand up so we all can see wot donkeys yew are, an the rest of yew, 'my fingers ar itchin' ... let us pray ...."

The prayers ended, the messages done, we filed slowly to our classrooms, Sade snapping at our heels, ruler waving, whacking us fiercely both, on the bums.

When the playtime bell rang Ewan and I bolted from the classroom like prisoners out of jail to gather in the playground with our seething, screaming, screeching, throbbing mass of friends.

"I'm on it," shouted Shidey. "I'll give yew ten to ide, an no out of school Ewan, or else yewr on it next time, right."

"Ee cant countu morrun ten," shouted Ewan laughing as he tugged me away in the direction of the playground shelter where we played under cover on days when it rained. "Up yer, eel never find us up yer," Ewan whispered as he, me following, shimmied up the twenty foot, metal green shelter pole onto the cold, grey slated roof where the wind pulled mercilessly at our pullovers and rearranged our already tangled hair.

"Yew sure we should be up yer Ewan?" I whispered nervously as we scrambled over the top out of Shidey's playground view.

"Yeah, iss in the school grouns in i, so's were alright in we, an ee carn see us."

Although we had escaped Shidey's attention, we hadn't Mr Sade's. Standing cup in hand in his headmaster's office window he had peered out just in time to catch a glimpse of our shiny short trousered backsides fast disappearing over the shelter roof top and down the other side.

"Jeesus I think ees seen us," whispered Ewan, momentarily meeting Sade's blazing eyes as he popped his head up over the roof top to see if Shidey was on his way. "Rhys, I think we're dead," his worst fears confirmed as the terrifying figure of Sade, stick in hand, appeared in the playground and marched towards the shelter pole. "Dew ee looks dangerous," said Ewan helpfully, "I don think ee wans to play ide an seek! ... Quick drop down the other side, he might not av noticed us," his urgency doing nothing to diminish my fear, or rid the unpleasant images of Sade and stick now flitting through my mind. It was too late, getting down was not as straightforward as getting up. We were stuck, and we froze, as the short, bellowed message that Ewan and I had heard a thousand times before travelled like a bolt of lightning up the metal shelter pole, tearing through the rooftop slate tiles and ripped into the recesses of our souls. "Office .... Now .... Both of Yew!"

Tight lipped and heads hung as if inspecting flea bites in the crannies of our toes, fists wrapped tightly, respectfully behind our backs, we stood, motionless, in abject misery at being caught, our shoulders fused in solidarity, a lifeline of companionship, strength and support, as evil Sade, ten feet tall and striding front of desk, laid into us with a venom overflowing with well-practised prose. "Yewr a disgrace, a disgrace to yewr school, yewr friends, yewr parents, to Pendre, do you yer me? What are yew? Yew are a ...."

"We wos ony playin idin Sir," interrupted Ewan," we woodn ave falln an got killd Sir ... wasn our fault we were up there anway Sir ... "

"Ewan, shut up. Yewr a disgrace, a big, massive, giant sized disgrace and a donkey to boot, what are yew? If I had a penny for every time it wasn't yewr fault I'd be the richest man in Pendre."

"It wan us Sir, it was Shidey's fault, ee said we coudn go out uf school to ide Sir, so we ad to go up."

With the kind of gut wrenching groan that suggested it would be unwise for Ewan to say more, Sade continued his speech. "And yewr a double disgrace Rhys, ees got no brain, but yew've half a one, if you had your brother's brain ..." he started ...

… "Hed have one an a alf Sir," chipped in Ewan, the act of bravery leading me later to give him half my Milky Way bar.

It was the last straw. He placed Ewan, then me, over his knee and whacked us three times a piece on our short grey trousered bums. His well-worn slipper delivering an accuracy born of knowing exactly where it was going and had been there many times before. We groaned, silently, as we slunk from Sade's dungeon, the ghosts of tears in our eyes, straining to look defiant as if we'd neither felt it nor even cared.

"Dew that urt," I finally gasped to Ewan, rubbin my bum with both hands once we were out of sight and earshot of Sade's dangerous lair, "ee must ave bin practisin is shot on iss missis."

"Yea, the grumpy bugger," said Ewan angrily, "ees good wi a slippper, but never mind eh, iss a pity for im. Praps iss the worry for is Mam thas made is badness a bit extru mean. Eel av is cumuppence in eaven one day you wait an see once John Baptist gets im."

It was the last of our adventures at Pendre junior school, indeed the end of our school friendship for some time to come. The hated 'eleven plus' examination was soon to tear me and Ewan, and countless others like us, cruelly apart. When the letters dropped to our doorsteps telling us who had 'passed' to the grammar and who had 'failed' to the secondary mod, a dark shadow swept over our households like the folds of Dracula's cloak, and we cried, like the day the chickens died, we cried, as the valleys cried, at the sadness and injustice of it all. Until a year later, on a re-sit which Ewan miraculously passed, our playground friendship was rekindled. And reunited, we again set about the task of avoiding education and teachers with renewed vigour and a much more accomplished expertise.

Chapter 6

Bopa's Choice

There was no choice, none at all. Coal or war, life, of a sort, if you were lucky, or death and glory. It was no choice at all. Garth, eighteen, chocolate eyed, bushy browed, bright as a miner's lamp, strong as a tallboy, school head boy, the world and every girl in Pendre at his feet; creeping, after school, and shop on Saturday nights, to Pendre top, to lie in the mountain heather with Mair, or Janice, or Bronwyn and laugh, and dream, of other times, other places, never seen, to be seen, and of justice and a better world. Coal or war, dust or death, it was no choice at all.

Or Glyn, two years younger, ten wiser, ruby eyed, rugby strong, rock steady, heart soft as melting snow, top of the form, dreaming, always dreaming, of better things and pretty girls, of love and life, to be, in London, another world, an architect, to paint and fashion the world and its people anew. Coal or war, life or death, there was no choice, no choice at all. Bopa, upright, radiant, chapel proper, soul of granite, shawled in goodness for family and Pendre friends; asking, never pleading, never begging, for her boys to be calm, to 'wait and see' tomorrow, for the love of God, stay at home; but to no avail. Coal or War, there was no choice, no choice at all. The die cast, for brothers bach and loved sister Mair, their lives, their futures, for Pendre, his people and for greater worthy goals, Rhys' mind set, bag packed, long before

Bopa's tears warmed and kissed the kitchen floor, to go, not to coal, but to war. There was no choice, no choice at all.

And so, in those forgotten times, while Glyn, back bowed, face blackened, spirit proud, scratched coal for Pendre and country beneath our cold valley floor, Bopa prayed and prayed and prayed, never failing, ever hoping, praying, praying, the pilot's prayer, for her boy, duty done, to fly safely home. Till the letter came, like angel's wings, and the shadows fell, and it was over; the Normandy skies claiming another soul, another son, brother, sister, lover's dreams. And Dad, satchel forever closed, grief buried deep in the dark black coal bowelled tombs of Rhymney, worked on, for coal and community and country, until the day that Bopa died. There was no choice at all.

Dad's shop, heart of Pendre, proud as a cathedral, small as a stable and as humble too; across the road chapel Bethel, its baleful, sometimes tuneful, hymn singing soul. Outside, its pavements scrubbed, hand polished, its windows shining bright, casting rainbows on pyramids of soap powders and pancakes, cornflakes and cat foods, Dad's Monday, constructed once monthly, 'displays for the day', all watching over corners of cobwebs, graveyards of dead creepy crawlies, spilled tea leaves and tinsels and out of reach wastelands of brittle wasp wings. And shelves, floor to ceiling, leaning backwards, never steady, dripping colour, drooping heavy beneath jars of sweets and meats, buckets and bananas, mops and marmalade, black bottled coffee, *Camp*, and dusty red boxes of Hornimans tea.

Two shop counters, glossed and tidied, re-built to splendour by Dad's willing but very un - handy hands. One creaking solid beneath a bell ringing brown money grabbing till, 'fresh in tomorrow' cream cakes, Tuesdays, fish on Fridays, and big as a Pembroke porpoise Megan's weighty leaning frame. And crowning glory, a giant fist of yellow speckled bread crumbed ham, cooked same day with secret ingredients - floating apple with fag ash 'for flavour' by Dad's same coloured nicotine hands - resting, nestling, waiting to meet its violent end by the hand turned, whirring, pit and pendulum, wheel slicing beast of a bacon machine, its speciality serving - fingertip and ham.

Outside - parsnips, sacked potatoes, caulis, wooden caged cabbages, and on Thursdays, old Joe's Missis, tired eyed Bett, resting like an idle miner against carefully painted black/green window walls. Dad's shop, heart of Pendre. Dad, Mam and helper born to smile till she died Megan, its pulse, life and soul - Pastors, counsellors, friends, neighbours, givers and takers of good and bad advice, together seeping, oozing, soothing, street binding ointments of solace, kindness, knowledge, blood of the valleys gossip and laughter - for the people of Pendre and all others who ventured in... To take home for free from that ever noisy, three people packed full Pendre shop that Dad had made his own.

And so he worked and worked, except Thursdays half days, like a pit head wheel, never still, never stopping; shop and more shop, Mam and Megan toiling, chatting, working, laughing, 'holding the fort' whenever he was away. But at the end of the day, his back aching, heart singing, he returned weary to Heddfan, to supper and slump, couch and tele, feet bowled and swimming in water and salts, to puff on woodbines, laugh and tell his children tales of the day.... There was no choice, for Dad, Mam (Dol to all who knew and loved her) or Megan, no choice, none at all.

"Sut mae Glyn - how are you today bach?" puffed Mrs Howells dragging her bandaged legs painfully slowly, up, over the black polished step past the resting caulis and into Dad's tiny shop, to lean precariously like a storm battered stork, against Dad's inside window frame. "Hows Dol, Glyn? Is er cold eny better? Yew look after that girl now Glyn, yew won find better in Pendre than that one ..."

"She's fine Mrs Howells ... be in later when the boys are gone to football an I'm stocking up. Are you ollright Mrs Howells..? Yew are looking a bit flushed ... yew shouldn be walking up Pendre ... send Tom ... get im off is backside ... or I'll deliver for yew ... just send yewr order up with one of the boys ... Yew sure yew are alright Mrs Howells? Ewan, get the stool for Mrs Howells...."

Mrs Howells, thin as a kipper, bent as a banana, fragile as a summer fly; fish on Fridays, cornflakes and half pound of Caerphilly on Saturdays and a 'few nice bits and pieces' extra for Tom's Sunday tea. Mrs Howells, smart as a tailor's hat, four foot nothing, every bit goodness and not a day under hundred and three, in my and Ewan's eyes......

"There yew are Mrs Owell ... how are yew Mrs Owell ... yew sit there Mrs Owell," chirped Ewan as he dragged the black wooden topped stool to the front of the counter to shove it indelicately behind Mrs Howell's slowly descending backside......

"Thank yew Ewan ... that's better ... How are yew Ewan? Rhys? Good boys Glyn ... lot of help for yew in the shop I espect?"

"Great elp Mrs Howells ... they'll be off to football in a bit."

"Is yewr cat orright Mrs Owell?" asked Ewan. "Ope so ... didn mean to urt im yesterday ... ee thought ee was a goalie ... played like a lion though ... bit unlucky im standing there reely as iss the first time Shidees scored for yers Mrs Owell, an anycase, I said i wan a goal cos i wen in off the cat ... Shidee said i counted ... cat didn seem to wan t play any more afer that Mrs Owell but I don think ee was urt ... ee made a good run up the wing after anyrate ..."

"Thank yew Ewan," interrupted Dad, "that's enough, just put Mrs Howells' stick there where she can reach it. Yew sure yew are ok Mrs Howells ... Mrs Howells? Ewan take Mrs Howell's arm ..."

"A bit faint I think Glyn ... thats all ... that hills steeper every time I walk it ... iss just a bit warm today thats all ... Ill be alright in a minit ...."

"Look, Ewan, get Mrs Howells' stick. Mrs Howells, yew cum out the back a minit. Iss cooler out there. I'll make yew a nice cup of tea. Yew can stay there till yewv got yewr breath back. Rhys, go and knock on Tom and tell im to get iss bum off the couch and bring iss van round, Mrs Howells is feeling a bit poorly ... and don stop to talk ... jus urry up."

"Oh no, no, Glyn, it'll pass," puffed Mrs Howells, "I'll be oright in a minit ... oh I am sorry to put yew to trouble Glyn."

"No trouble Mrs Howell," soothed Dad, taking her fragile arm and leading, half carrying her weightless frame, slowly, Ewan following stick in hand, to the dark back-room store to rest amongst the box towers of butter, *Daz*, beans, crisps, everything, waiting to find its way front of house to fill the spaces in Dad's overflowing store.

"There, sit there, Mrs Howells, iss a bit cooler there," Dad cooed as he gently lowered Mr Howells downwards and she slithered, limp languid, like a captured cat, straight through his arms, missing the patched armchair to rest at his feet amongst the boxes on the black, red rose carpet of the storeroom floor....

"Mrs Howells!" croaked Dad.

"Dew, shes gon an died Mr Davies, look at that, dead as a blue-bottle Mr Davies, just like that Mr Davies, never seen a dead person live before Mr Davies ... dew, a body, Mr Davies ..."

"Ewan, shut up, she's fainted that's all, give me a hand ..."

"No Mr Davies, look at her teeth Mr Davies, Jack says wen their teeth cums out theys dead as nails Mr Davies ... sheel be goin stiff in a minit I spect Mr Davies, bettu straigten er out or else theyll never get er in the box ..."

"EWAN ... shut up", threatened Dad, as he pulled Mrs Howells into the arms of the waiting armchair. "She's fainted, that's all, now give me a hand. Go out the front and tell me when you see Tom's van comin. Ewan, take her stick. I'll carry Mrs Howells to the front in a minit, go on Ewan, do as yew are told ..."

"I'll get some money from the till first Mr Davies."

"Lord above Ewan, we don't need money ... what d'we need money for ..."

"er eyes Mr Davies ... yewv gota put money on er eyes Mr Davies ... seen it on the tele ... stops um falling out I spect ... seen it on Dixon Doc Green ... Jack says if theyr teeth an eyes fall out Mr Davies theyv ad it."

"Ewan", sighed Dad desperately, "just go to the front and tell me when Tom's van's comin ..."

"Oright Mr Davies, sure yew can manage er?"

With the ease of a collier lifting a bag of dried beans Dad hauled Mrs Howells into his arms and carried her forward, gently, past the nestling cabbages, through to the front of the shop to wait the arrival of Tom's grey, one time butcher's, van ...

"Yer ee cums Mr Davies, they'll be yer in a minit ... fetch er out."

Dad stepped outside ....

"Ello Mr Davies," sang Lill as Dad stumbled towards Tom's open van door, "oh, good God, is that Mrs Howells, Mr Davies, oh thas terrible Mr Davies, I was ony saying to my Dai the other day how I thought she was a bit poorly Mr Davies and now she's gone, Lord rest her soul, an me first to know Mr Davies, oh thas terrible for er Tom Mr Davies ..."

Talk of Pendre, gossip of Wales, Lill, once of pit laundry and part time wife of Dai ball and chain - "Jack says can't keep the buggu down off the table after ees ad a couple of pints in im ... needs a ruddy ball an chain to keep im on the floor and stop im from is awful cronin, dull bugger ..." - and Dad's least favourite customers of the day.

"Yes ... very sad Lill," sighed Dad, the look of a grieving collier etched convincingly across his brow, Mrs Howells motionless in arms. "Found er this mornin, out the back in a packit of Smiths, must av been in there all night poor soul ... aftu the bag of salt I spect ... sad... too much for er at er age, still we've all got to go sometime .... Left a note in the salt though saying she was sorry for the trouble. Lovely lady, Lill, be badly missed ... See you in a minute Lill, er Tom's yere to take er away ... have to hurry Lill, I spect they'll ave to get lots of water into er quick before they bury er to get rid of the salt, else she'll go rusty from the inside .... Pity eh, what a way to go."

With a packet of cornflakes and a nice piece of Caerphilly for Tom's Sunday tea tucked safely beside her, Mrs Howells was gently laid to rest in the front of Tom's waiting van. With a scowl for Tom and a "take her home quick", we watched as the van lurched away. As they disappeared around Pendre bend Dad lit a woodbine, smoothed his apron and prepared for the next task of the day.

"See you later Mr Davies," chanted Ewan as we ran from the shop to head for the 'reck' to play another under 14s, Saturday afternoon football game, and Mam, rosy fresh from her walk from Heddfan, and two doors down the road Megan, laughing, rolled into position for their afternoon shift. Shelf filling, chatting, laughing, sooth saying while covering for Dad released to 'Cash n

Carry' for fag and chat and load his van to overflowing with everything needed to replenish his bowed and over loaded shelves. "Alright Meg? ... Bill an boys alright ...?" beamed Dol as Meg pulled on her apron ...

"Fine Dol bright as daisies ... lorries not right though ... Bill' will av it sorted by Monday ... should see the state of is overalls though, underneath that lorry all day long, black, blue, few white spots ... like a ruddy miner's bum ... like to see that ruddy *Persil* man on the tele get the stains off my Bill's backside. Where we goona start then Dol? You do the sweets or me? Oh dew, watch out Dol, yer cums Stopesees, less ide quick ... I don wana serve the mean creature, havn got the time for im since ee give my Bill a parkin tickit in Trefan for smokin with a sanwich on yellow lines ... Look at im, six foot six of gristle and a not a pea brain in iss ead. Owd ee get a job in the Police eh? I don know... all like im I bet. Get the bananas out Dol, I spect eel be wantin wun for iss tea... eats um sideways ... ony mouth in Pendre can do that .... Oh, hello Mr Stopes, how are yew today ... lovely to see yew ... yewr Mary orright?"

"Fine Meg ..."

"Any criminals out there today Mr Stopes? ... Not with yew about I spect ... dangrus times though eh ... a couple of thu buggus in my gardn last night ... tried to pinch my drawers off the line ... found um dead this mornin ... smuthud .... wanna see the evidence?"

"Couple of bananas Dol pleas" ordered Stopes, ignoring Meg's playful taunt, "an a custard ... thas all for now ..."

"Right Mr Stopes," croaked Mam, barely able to contain the laughter breaking from her smile.

"Yewr Rhys oright Dol? ... I'd watch who ee angs round with ... My advice ... If yew dont mind me sayin ... Ees a good boy, if ee stops off the roofs .... all I say, keep an eye on im, spends too much time with that bad crowd if yew ask me - you know who I mean ...."

"That'll be one and six Mr Stopes, please, good of you to think of im Mr Stopes ... I'll hav a word ... ees a good boy though ... I'll keep an eye on im. Say ello to Mary for me ... see her in chapel tomorrow I espect ... Enjoy your tart now, nice fresh one that ...."

"Dew Dol, that man kills me," laughed Meg as she re-emerged from behind the counter where she'd crouched, doubled, to hide her rumbling laughter from the wrath of Pendre's criminal fighting force. "That poor girl Mary, Dol - howd she live with im eh, I don know. They says ee sleeps with iss helmut on in case there's n emergency ... says Mary's never seen the top of is head ... iss gotta be betta thun the bottom ... None so queer eh. You do the apples Dol, I'll do the sweets, won be many in this afternoon I spect, iss too nice.... Hello Jan ... Binney... ave a sit on the stool ... what can we do for you? .... Dol I'll serve these, yew carry on ... Jan, bit of ham is it? ...

Chapter 7

Lord Be Praised

"Didn spect to see yew in chapel tonight Ewan," I beamed, as Ewan and Jack strode up the gravelled pathway towards the chapel doors. "O'right Rhys … Mr Davies?" Jack mumbled as he brushed past the grey suited deacons and on, through the inside swinging doors and seated himself at the edge of the pock marked wooden pew beneath the giant white/brown round face of the black handed ticking clock, overhanging on the wall.

"No, iss Jack ... says ee wants a few words with the Almighty ... why iss coupons en cumin up I spect ... an Mrs Jones won let im stay late since ee did er pipes and er goins keep cumin up in er garden ... Jack says the miserable buggu should be grateful ... er roses av nevu been bettu ... an ee en a plummer anyrate ... says shee shouldn be makin the garden smell so bad. Anyrate", Ewan whispered, loudly, as we sidled into position against the sweet carrying pockets of Ewan's silent, head bowed, solemn Uncle Jack, "whose preachin tonight ?"

"Mrs Copsley I think ..."

"O dew ir aint is i .... we'll be yer till Tuesday ... an I don wana be late, the Pladiums on an I wana see the jackpot .... Rhys, go an tell yer Dad to play the ims double quick - ee won wanna be yer all night, eel be dyin for a fag ..."

"Rhys, Ewan ... eisht," poked Mam, seated strategically behind us with Bessy, Edie and Gran, austere, upright, watching soldiers. Mrs Copsley, her neckless head floating like a bobbin apple inches visible above the pulpit stand, her torso motionless as if set in concrete to the platform floor, took a deep breath and began her evening prayer....

"Bet yew how many times she says 'Lord', Rhys, yew know what she's like ... Lord above, Lord below, Lord down the pan, Lord everywhere you look with er ... a tannu on twenty-six ..."

"Fifty ... an yew avn got a tannu anyrate ..."

"Rhys ... Ewan ... shut it," hissed Mam ...

"Lord .... Let us pray ...."

With Ewan's fingers deep mining wool fluffed mintos from the pockets of Jack's coat, our eyes fixed glued to the chapel floor, and Dad rustling restlessly at the chapel organ dying for a fag, the clock ticked time away to the start of the Pladium show as Mrs Copsley laid into her sermon with the vigour and force of a Goliath, belying her small but solid frame of four foot by four ... "And the Lord Almighty came to them in a dream and said, 'take my message to other lands', the good Lord be praised ... Lord bless us ...."

"Fifteen Rhys ..."

"An ten good men of the village packed their Mules and headed north to the high mountains, laden with our good Lord's precious words .... and they climbed, higher and higher along the rocky track, and as the track became narrow ... the Lord gave them strength ... an narrower ... Lord be praised ...."

"Lost count Ewan ... giss a sweet off Jack ..."

"...an higher until the track became a treacherous pathway, but the Lord was with them ... 'Shall we go on?' they cried .... the track narrowed still ... Lord be praised ... until the first man toppled, his mule and his soul falling to a rocky grave .... Lord have mercy ... 'Shall we go on?' they cried .... and they did ... until the second man toppled .... Lord rest his good soul ...."

"Thas a tannu yew ow me Ewan ..."

"'Shall we go on?' they cried .... and they did ... until only one man and his weary mule remained ....

"My dear friends," cried Mrs Copsley, tears streaming from her eyes, "there is a message here, a message here for us all .... What was our good Lord trying to tell these ten brave men?" ....

Silence .... as the head bowed congregation take stock of this tragic, mournful tale ... and more silence ... until ... unable to bear the cross of silence hanging heavy in the air, Jack rises .... and bellows ...

"Go ome an take the ruddy low road Mrs Copsley yew ask me." Before Mrs Copsley could deliver true enlightenment to our tired but willing souls ...

"No ... Jack ... NO ... Lord have mercy on - "

THUMP.... the dull thud on the outside chapel door reverberated through the congregation like dynamite breaking a new seam of coal, jolting Mr Lewis tidy from his noisy, dribbling snooze, and halting Mrs Copsley momentarily from her flow of Lordly reasons why mules and men had chosen wisely to go steadfastly on ...

"Iss those ruddy boys muckin about outside again," whispered Jack. "Ewan, Rhys, cum with me." Sidling off the bench, into the chapel aisle, out past Mrs Copsley and the watching congregation, we tiptoed through the vestry doorway and into the kitchen hall ....

"See if there's a buckit under there Rhys'" Jack whispered pointing to the cupboard beneath the vestry sink .... "Ay ... thatll do ... Fill it with water Ewan ... leave it a bit empty I'll add somthin a bit special in a minit .... don make a noise now ..."

The bucket nearly full and positioned centre of the vestry floor, Jack turned away, unbuttoned his flies, aimed, peed, and filled it full...

"Right, now follow me, an no noise ... don wana disturb Mrs Copsley, I spect shes arf way up the ruddy Mountain again by now ..."

As we crept past the solemn congregation their heads solemnly bowed, all eyes shifted side wards to stare at the steaming bucket ceremony creeping in tandem quietly back down the aisle. Jack turned, mouthed to Mrs Copsley ...

"Christenin Mrs Copsley ... don stop ... back in a minit I spect ..." and we hastened onwards, like good Christian soldiers, out of the chapel into the entrance hall toward the visitors waiting outside. Raising the bucket menacingly in his strong and steady hands, Jack whispered, "Right, wen I nod ... Ewan, Rhys - get those doors open an duck, if yew don wana get a taste of wat I ad down the Stute last night. Right ... one ... two ... three ..."

As Ewan and I threw ourselves wildly against the oak shiny brown chapel doors, flinging both open wide, Jack, eyes blazing, black yellow teeth flashing, bellowed, "Tell yer Mams yewv been christened yer buggus," and cast his Christenin cocktail over the unsuspecting 'ooligans', mouths agape, outside. As the warm, sweet smelling cider cocktail enveloped their fright frozen bodies like shite hitting a coal wall fan, Jack again leapt forward, bucket waving. "Catch yew yer again yew maggots an Ill take yew thro the ruddy crewsifiction as well … Ill be up later to av a word with yu Dads … now buggur off … sorry God ….”

Driven less by the fear of the Almighty than the sight of Jack's teeth and his flying, black silver toed pit boots, the boys squelching wet, hared down the pathway and out of the chapel grounds and up Pendre hill like whippets off a block. As they disappeared from sight Jack gently pulled the chapel door closed behind and whispered, "Best not go back in there to disturb Mrs Copsley eh bach? I spect shell be wantin a bit of quiet to get them mules round them narrow bends ... Say evnin to Dol and Mr Davies for me will yew Rhys," and grinning, he strolled off down the chapel pathway, rolled a woodbine and went on his way.

With the bucket rested empty at the side of the chapel wall and the sounds of '*Will Your Anchor Hold*' drifting soothingly through the holes in the stained glass windowed doors, Ewan and I leapt the chapel wall, ran across the fields to Heddfan, kicked off our wet shoes and settled in front of tele to watch the Pladium, all alone. With three sugared Welsh cakes and a cup of warm tea, we laughed together as we rehearsed the very good Lordly reasons why Sian and Ieuan had sadly to stay in chapel singing, while we and Jack just had to go home. There was no choice, none at all.

Chapter 8

The Band

"We need a group Rhys," blurted Ewan, bored, the following Saturday as we sat on the garage driveway listening to his sister's tranny that he'd borrowed on loan. "Ieuans got one ... iss good ... like the Beatles ... we could be the Beachboys ... get some money ..."

"Yeah ... good idea Ewan ... a group ... one of yewr best Ewan ... ow we gonna be a group eh ... don be so daft .... We carn play anythin, we carn sing and we en got enywhere to practise ... so how we gonna be a group eh?"

"Yew cun play 'risin sun' on the the guitar ... thas reely good ... and Jack says eel get me a drum if I practise in the garrige ... itll be good ... Sian can sing ... she cun be wos er name ... blonde air ... no socks ... Sandy Opkins .... an Owells cun be base gitar ... ees got one and the girls like im cos ee looks likes one of them Animals ..."

"Ee is n animal ... an ee won wana play with us less we pay im, an av yew erd Sian sing ... the cats better thun er ..."

"Anyrate," continued Ewan undeterred, "we got to now I told Jack wed do it ..."

"Do what Ewan...!?"

"The New Yer's Miners do ... Jack says theyv got a group for the main bit, 'Valleys Death' or sumut ... but ee thinks theys a bit eavy for the little uns so ee wants someut to cheer um up aftu with some nice songs ... ony need three or four ee said ... an eel pay us ...."

"God elp us Ewan ... yew need yewr ed read ... how we gonna do that ... ow cun we play at the Miners ... theres undreds of um there ... wed be laughed off the stage ..."

"Don be stewpid," sighed Ewan, as always disappointed at my lack of ambition and faith in his grand plans, "iss easy ... them groups on the tele carn sing eny bettu than us ... Yewve erd Tom Dylan ..."

"Bob ..."

"Yeah, im, ees useless ... an e en got any group ... iss no problem.... Yew ask Sian an I'll get Owells.... "

That Monday, as Owells pinned fat 'stumpy' Williams to the rust red prison railings of Pendre Grammar's lower playground wall, Ewan raised the delicate matter with him of whether he would like to enjoy a life of stardom, wealth and women by joining our newly formed rock group.

"Dyou wanu join a group then Owells ... Rhys'n me ave startid one .... iss good ... gonna be famus ... yew cun be in it if yewwant ..."

"Piss off Ewan. Wouldn be seen dead with yew ..."

"Right ... yeah ...." ignoring this 'friendly' remonstration at a safe distance from Owells' endeavour to stretch the strap of Stumpy's leather satchel from his neck to the school gate post.

"We've got a bookin ... the Miners ... Jack said therell be undreds there ... yer bound to be spotted ... Jack says therll be a scouts from all ovu thu place ... Hewy Cream from the Pladiums cumin ... an ..."

"Wos i called then...?"

"Avn reely got a name yet ... but Rhys said somut like ....'Valley Drizzle' ..."

"Ruddy 'Wet Spazzees' would be bettu for yew lot ... yew cretins carn play anythin anyway."

"Oh cum on Owells .... iss ony for wunce ... an Jack says eel pay us ...."

"Ow much?" chipped in Owells, his interest at last secured.

"Arf a quid ... if we do three songs proper ..."

"Where yew gonna practise then?"

"Jacks garrige ... after school tomorrow ... orright?"

"Ten bob... Right. Once. An I dun av to stand by yew or Rhys."

"Right ... see you there then ... bout six ... after tea."

That same evening, after school, I broached the matter with Sian as she lay rolled on the couch with Tiddles, as Ieuan thumped out Beatles numbers on the piano out the back.

"Won wun of these Sian?" a black an white minto held out in my hand.

"Yeah ... right ... what dyou wan Rhys?"

"Nuthin ... just that ..."

"Whad dyu wan Rhys ...?"

"Do us a favour sis ... "

"No."

"Oh go on Sian - I en told yew what it iss yet ..."

"No ... dun won a know."

"Yew ow me one."

"Oh yeah ... ows that then ...."

"Didn tell Mam where me an Ewan saw yew and Berwyn on Sunday did we?"

"What d'y wan Rhys .... yew say a word about me an Berwyn an yewr dead ... right?"

"Just wont yew to sing a couple of songs thas all ... me an Ewan startid a group an we thought yew could be in i ... yew would be good ..."

"NO .... Forget it."

"Oh cum on Sian ... Id do it for yew ... an theres money ..."

Sian, sitting up, taking her eyes off the box.

"Oh yeh... ow much ... an where yew gonna get money from?"

"Ewans got us a bookin at the Miners do ... after Christmas ... ony got to do a couple of songs ... and we need a singu ... and Jack says eel give us ten bob each ... itll be good ... Berwyn can cum ... he'll think yewr a star ..."

"Two songs ...?"

"Well maybe three ..."

"I en practisin ... If yew gi me thu songs to learn Ill av a look ... but I en going near Ewan on no stage right ... an yew tell Mam about me an Berwyn an is off ... right?"

With Howells signed for stardom for a ten bob note and Sian's deal, never to be seen near Ewan or me except for an hour on stage, no more, at the Miners annual do and no turnin up 'ever' for practice ever, 'at all', we were more than ready for Maerdy's annual do. And so, with Ewan kitted with silver red drum kit - a shilling from a Save the Children stall - and Howells a plastic comb and three-string bass guitar, we practiced, loudly, no Sian, in Ewan's garage, once only, three songs, *Sloop John B, Rising Sun* and our grand finale, the Beatles *Nowhere Man*. If as expected the crowd should call for more, we would play the same again. "Told you we could do it Rhys, jus don go mad with the comb Howells thas all." We were heading inexorably upwards towards stardom and a life of well-deserved fame. In Ewan's eyes, we would soon be sharing a caravan with the valley's one and only other decent singer, "the one tha sings bout is omes a green valley, I think is names Tom Stones."

A cacophony of children's laughter, mingled with the echoes of 'Valley Death's third encore, greeted us as we quietly crept on stage. Sian positioned herself front of house, nervously fighting the bean pole thin, black capped microphone towering over her, six feet tall. Ewan seated centre back, twirled his drumsticks wildly while spinning dizzily on his drum kit stool. Howells, clutching his base guitar, delicately re-arranged his Roy Orbinson wide dark glasses while smoothing his Vaseline laden greased back hair. I stood as near the curtains as was decent in case we needed rapidly to get away. As the lights dimmed, we faced the swaying seated children packed tightly on the floor, their parents standing, drinking, chatting, laughing, eagerly awaiting the melodies that would mark a happy ending to Maerdy's Miners' New Year 'do'.

As the lights dimmed and the crowd hushed, Ewan leapt to his feet and drumsticks waving, launched suddenly, like a wounded wolf howling in despair, alone into our chosen first song and gateway to stardom, the Animals

Rising Sun....... ending his rendition as abruptly as it had begun, but with a flourishing drum roll. As the sound of stunned, whispering, polite applause dimmed, Howells turned to Ewan, "Yew cretin ... wait for us." Ewan undimmed then launched into our second number - *Sloop John B* - again alone ... "Ewan, Ewan!!" screamed Sian, "Shut up!!!" to no avail, as we desperately tried to join him in his solo refrain.

The heat of the stage was now taking its toll and Howell's scarecrow body began swaying strangely as his glasses drooped to the edge of his nose. And as Howells groaned and Sian, fright frozen static to the wooden stage floor, grimly mumbled what she could recall of the words to *Sloop John B*, Ewan drummed on wildly, oblivious to the numbing effects of our music on the restless children below. Our second number over to the sound of no applause, the crowd waited nervously in fear that there should be more. As we waited, and waited, for Sian to launch our grand finale, Valley Drizzle's unique version of the Beatles *Nowhere Man*, a silence descended over the auditorium like a blanket over a corpse. "Ow was I supposed to remember all those words eh when I got things to do eh ... an sing over yewr awful noise," said Sian a little later," I en a jenius ... an I didn wanna be in yewr yewsluss group anyrate."

With the rising tension becoming too much for Ewan to bear, he launched again, spontaneously, into a demented, ear piercing drum roll, arms flailing like windmill's arms in an Aberystwyth storm. "Unusual ... no ... very unusual," said Mrs Thomas piano later, "for the ballad of *Nowhere Man* ..."

As the lights came up, Ewan, beaming proudly, strode to the front of stage to receive his encore, as behind him we watched the staring children, mouths open, deathly silent, legs crossed tightly on the cold wooden floor, turn desperately, despairingly, to their dumbstruck parents, eyes pleading, 'please ... please ... Mam ... Dad ... please ... please ... No More!'

As the curtains fell on our short career as a pop group and Ewan's as a star, backstage Jack clutched at Ewan's waving drumsticks and laughed. "Yew were supposed to cheer the buggus up not kill um with depreshun yew ruddy idiuts ... Still, never mind eh - they needed shutin up after that ruddy Death lot ... never erd such a noise in my life before ... so I spose yewr worth yer ten shillings ... but I don think yewll be featuring top o th bill next yer ... do yew?" And with that, he led us through the back door exit, past angry parents, towards his waiting van outside.

Quietly, we loaded Ewan's drum and drumsticks into the back of Jack's old van. Crestfallen, our singing careers over, we headed for home. As Sian and Owells slumped like sacked potatoes against the cold tin grey van wall, grumpily blaming each other for their short- lived taste of fame, Ewan shot upright with the rhythm of the bouncing van. "Armony ... thas where we wen wrong ... din av enuf armony in John B ... thas wo wos wrong ...."

"Didn av any bloody thing in *Nowhere Man*," mumbled Jack.

"No! 'Thas wot Mrs Thomas piano said. Wunce we got armony therll be no stoppin us ...." And with that he fell silent, smiling, dreaming of fame and stardom, Pendre's answer to the Animals, the Beatles, the Beachboys - Valley Drizzle, the valley's one and only band.

Chapter 9

Dangerous Times

There was no choice, none at all... thumped in French, Mondays; ignored or chalked in Maths, Tuesdays; ridiculed and abused in Geology, Wednesdays; life threatened in Science, Thursdays; terrorised in Games, Fridays; the people's curriculum, schooling for getting on and out, to leave our valleys, our country, our home. There was no choice, none at all. Pendre Grammar, pride of the valleys, hewn from a rock face, built on a hillside, grey as a castle, cold as a dungeon, brutal as a warrior and nice as mustard too; its hated, unconvincing, much practised mantra 'do as I say boy, not what I cruelly do'. A 'good education', while down the road secondary modern, mammon, no education, or none worth speaking of at all, or so we were told...

"Right you boys ... books out ... page 24 ... homework ... iss called Geology ... let's see what you've done ..."

As Ewan sketched bombers and I picked players for Saturday's football game, we sat, huddled, shoulders and heads together, eyes down, at the back of the room, desperately trying to avoid teacher Yanto's piercing gaze. Yanto, big as a polar bear, without any hair, dangerous to look at and good as dead if caught in his stare .... always leaning backwards, pacing forwards, front of blackboard, never smiling, always striding, black caped sentry from hell, on this occasion, two rocks held lightly in the centre of his gangly outstretched hands.

"Ewan ... two minerals here boy ... what can you tell me about them?"

"Nice ones Sir."

"Excellent Ewan, remarkable ... What else?"

"Wuns a bit round an ruff Sir ..."

"Yes ..."

"The other wuns a bit rounder and ruffer Sir ..."

"Yewr a genius Ewan ... wot else Davies?"

"That wuns white Sir, that wuns a bit browner Sir ..."

"Magnificent Davies ... it makes teaching worthwhile .... Wot did we do for homework last night boy... waste of time asking I suppose ... Which one of these is the heavier ...?"

Hands dart up, Ewan's and mine, heads and hands straight down, locked beneath the table, praying desperately, despairingly for the lesson to end.

"Ewan?"

"Looks bout thu same to me Sir ..."

"Davies ...?"

"Same Sir ... same size Sir ... the white wun ... no the brown wun Sir ... looks a bit eavier Sir ..."

"They are the same size boy ... did you open yewr homework book last night ... Ewan?"

"Looks bout the same to me Sir," dazzled by Yanto's dullness. "Don mattu does i Sir if they fits in yer bag ..."

"Ewan, yewr a donkey of the first order boy .... Let me put it this way ... let's say we have here yewr and Davies' brains on the table in front of us ... both the same size .... which is the heavier...?'

Hands shoot up ... "Philpotts?"

"Trick question Sir ...."

"Why's that Philpotts?"

"Ewan's got no brain Sir ..."

"Thank you boy ..."

"Let's say Ewan's brain has three ingredients - sawdust, footballs and crayons ... Davies' has four ingredients - sawdust, footballs, Mary Thomas and a tiny bit of grey matter ... Which might be the heavier... Ewan?"

"Rhys' Sir"...

"Why's that Ewan?"

"S'got more bits in it Sir ..."

"Right Ewan ... density. Page 15. Homework ... did yew look at it boy?"

"Forgot Sir ... Sir duss that mean Rhys is densu thun me then Sir?"

"Ewan ... the mornin fog's not as dense as yew, or Davies. Davies ... tell us something useful ... what did yew study last night boy ... Tell us the score."

"Two one Sir."

"We have learnt something class. Davies has contributed to our education ... the score for Cardiff City last night was two one ... the sum total of yewr knowledge boy ... I'll see if they do 'O' levels in John Toshack for yew Davies. Yew are a donkey. That table is more useful than yew ... yew and Ewan ... come out the front the pair of yew and sit there ... yewr a waste of time."

There was no choice... none at all.

Science, Thursdays, 'in the war Watkins', ten feet massive, head like a tombstone, no neck at all. Ewan says "they dropped im out of u plane on a secret mission ... says ee was a Paratrooper ... dull buggu thought it'd be safer if ee landed on iss ead, thas whys ees got no neck. No wundu they surrendud seein im ... thought if theres more like im ... wouldn stand a chance ... Walesis secret weapon ...." Watkins. Never destined to be my, Ewan's, nor even brainy boffin Phillpotts' choice of best friend.

"Get im in yer Rhys ... ees rottin to the floor out there ... I've got something useful for im an yew to do," boomed Watkins, one drab science morning.

Ewan's usual position in science was face beaming, eyes shining, peering intently through the tiny square glass window that centred the top of the chemistry lab door; standing tip toe, outside looking in, or sitting knees to chin on the grimy carpet floor. He grimaced as I opened the door and called him in to sit beside me. "Wos he want Rhys ... I don wona come in ..." he whispered as we took our places behind the most remote lab bench and instantly leaned forward to fiddle the gas taps and catch the watery drippers falling languidly to their white basined graveyard end. Heads together, we waited, with fearful certainty, for Watkins' next nasty command.

"Out yer the pair of yew ..." pointing to beside him.

"We are going to go over what we did last week ... No point in asking yew two is there ... hands up ....

Yes Williams?"

"Combustion Sir."

"Good Williams ... combustion ... This week we are going to demonstrate what that means. Page 44 .... Homework ... we shall see the explosive, heat and warming effects of combining certain substances with water and air."

Growls ...

"Yew two ..." staring unnaturally at Ewan and me.

"Yes Sir" ... in harmony ... glued to the spot ...

"Don move ... don touch ... don think ... or else ... yer me?"

"Yes Sir."

Watkins walks to the mysterious dark room, papered with meaningless symbols on wall hanging charts, past jars of orange pink-red powders, cracked/creased stretched rubber tubes, black burners and white bowls, towards the padlocked glass cabinet where Ewan says lethal poisons are kept for killing dead frogs, and carefully, slowly, pulls out a giant sweet jar, red lidded for danger, packed tightly with silk solid lumps of grey cotton wool. He returns, slowly, as if walking barefooted on glass, to behind the raised work bench at the front of class.

"Ewan, Davies ... cum up yer," pointing to the space immediately beside him. "The rest of yew ... get up the back ... leave your papers, yew won't need them for a minit ... an when I say down, yew get down behind the bench ... Right? ... Understood? Right, Ewan, Davies, listen to me carefully ... When I say ... Davies, yew will unscrew this lid ... and yew will hold the jar ... Ewan yew will take this tongs and yew will carefully remove a small piece of this grey substance from the jar ... Yew will then place it in this crucible ... that is a bowl to yew Davies ... of water. Davies yew will replace the lid firmly on the jar ... and then you stand back ... I shall be standing right over there ... is that clear?"

"Sir ..." pleaded Ewan.

"Yes Ewan …?"

"Yew carn do that Sir..."

"Why not boy?"

"Iss dangrus sur ... we'll be killd Sir ..."

"Quiet boy... think of it as yewr contribution to science."

"Sir ..."

"Davies?"

"Carn do it Sir ..."

"Why not Davies ? I'd say yew were ideal for the job."

"Sir ... if I'm killd Sir we avn got a substitute on Saturday Sir ... an Ewanll ave to play an ees uselus in goals Sir ... ask Shidey Sir ... eel do it ..."

"Quiet boy ... Do as yewr told."

As Watkins retreated to the side of the room, Shidey and the rest of class crouched low, peering from behind the back benches, smiling, silent, watching the pantomime unfold …

"Right ... unscrew the lid Davies."

Hands quivering, pulling at the red lidded jar, Ewan grasped the silver tongs and reached deeply into the red lidded jar. As he does, he whispers,

"Rhys less do the lot," and removes the full contents and dumps it unceremoniously, overflowing, into the waiting grey white crucible bowl ...

Silence ...

More silence ....

Eyes fixed, staring, waiting the unknown ...

WOOMPH ...

Sparks, dust, muck fly from the crucible like the black menace from Lloyd Herbert's coal lorry exhaust, leaving me and Ewan standing, startled, mouths open, smiling, faces covered in soot.

"Bluddy ell Sir that was ruddy brilliunt," gasped Ewan as the dust settled on the wooden bench. "Less do it again ... outside Itlers offis, thatll shake the buggu up ..."

Watkins, eyes blazin, white coat flowing, Einstein on speed, strides forward, leaning backwards and wrests the jar, forever cracked useless, and the black charcoaled tongs, from Ewan's soot blackened hands, and spills his nasty venom on Ewan and me.

"Yew stewpid stewpid boys ... Ewan ... I said a small bit ... didn yew yer me? ...That is it now, the yers supply gone because of yewr stupidity ... an ow dare yew swear in class? .... Outside the pair of yew... Ill see yew both in my office after school ... Clean yewrself up boy, and yew Davies ... yew can join im outside till the end of the lesson ... yew stewpid, stewpid, stewpid boys ..."

Strangely, Ewan took to science after his experiment with the tongs, but not with Watkins who, for some inexplicable reason, was never seen again. Whether he was "taken away by people in white coats who en scientists to study in a ome", the nub of Ewan's authoritative claim, or Shidey's, that "eed gone with iss Bunsen burners to Africa to slice earthworms and teach the poor people who were dullu than im", we never would know; but after Watkins, neither science nor Ewan were ever quite the same again.

Chapter 10

A Valley Song

"Yew cumin swimmin tonight?" called Ewan as we parted to go to Maths. Ewan in 'remedial' me in CSE. "Dadll pick us up at the bus stop after school, four o clock ... iss is alf day ... see yew after RE ... right ... meet yew at the gates. Joclyn will be there ... she'll show us how to swim like a rissole ... an you can get Shidey back for givin your hat to his cat ... Did yew get the sick off ... drown im if I was yew ... an is cat."

Thursdays, half days, Empire-pool swimming days. Dad's weekly outin treat for his kids and their friends.

Van doors open, Mam and Dad beaming, open arm greeting at the front of the school. We pile in. Packed to overflowing, Ewan, Ieuan, Sian, Joclyn, Shidey, sardine squashed in the back of the van. Mam, knitting, tucked beside Dad up front, smiling, chatting, resting, contented, the world at its best with happy kids in hand .... Hours later, tired and happy, laughing hungry, hair dripping, towels sopping, pie and milky bar puddins held tightly in our greasy chip warmed hands, together we sing, 'round the mountin', 'ten green bottles', happy as Larrys, creeping slowly, like Joe's old greyhound, through the black night darkness up and over the steep mountain road, on our way home ....

"What if we stop Dol, an av a look at that new super-store in Taibach? Theyr all talkin about it ... they say iss huge ... big as Maerdy... got everythin in one ... stock the lot ... apparently iss the firstn biggest in Wales ... iss not far off the road ... We'll av a look eh, wont be in there long?"

"That'll be nice Glyn ..." sighed Mam. "I'll keep kids quiet while you're gone" ....

"That was quick love ..." Half an hour later, the van jam packed full with 'Anchor' butter packed tightly between our squashed up knees, we again rolled slowly on the long road home. Dad couched in silence, gaze fixed forward, face unsmiling, hands clasped tightly to the pockmarked orange plastic leather steering wheel.

"Dew Dol, I can't buy it that cheap from the warehouse ... I had no idea ... An iss all like that Dol ... what'll we do?"

"It'll be ok Glyn ... it'll be ok ...." soothed Mam.

The future ... writ large in a box of butter.

Shuttered windows,

broken grocers,

empty chapels,

political wastelands,

valleys green

turning pink

then blackened blue

There was no choice, for Dad and his people, his valley …

No choice for any of us … none at all.

But I've no sad tale to tell, not now anyway. Even when the shadows fall and we again talk of daft, mad, flew off the roof with a bucket on his head, Dafydd Ewan and of loved ones lost. Mam, doll tiny, tough as a diamond, soft as an angel, ground from the country to work till she died, with tireless, unerring devotion to her children and everyone else except her own lonely soul. And Dad, massive, rock like, mind and wisdom to match, Welsh to the marrow, mined from the valleys for the valleys, front of house grocer, miner in his day; driven, never single minded, by dreams of how much better his neighbours', his valley's, his country's lot, really ought to be; and by love, for family, friends, and community, loyally served, to a tragic, sad, but never bitter end. His life and the valleys, inextricably intertwined. We'll not weep. That wasn't his, or our way.

I've no sad tale to tell, but a fine, glad, happy story, first, of the beginning of the day.

The End

Acknowledgements

My eternal gratitude goes to:

My loving, ever patient and forgiving parents, Gwyn and Dorothy, for making all things seem possible and permissible.

My precious family, Jan, Rhianedd, Ceryn, Phil, Erin, Gwyn and Osian, for providing daily reminders of all that is good and joyous in life.

Loving sister Lynne, and Arwyn, long suffering brother Rhys, and Carol for your painstaking proofreading of Wenglish.

Hywel Evans, whose wonderful creative endeavour and stubborn persistence brought this story to fruition.

Richard Ross for so vividly capturing times past.

Russell Gomer for brilliantly echoing the voices of the Valleys for the audio book.

And above all, Ewan and the good, kind, decent people of the Rhymney valley.

... And Silver. Truly a remarkable orse.

Printed in Great Britain
by Amazon